MIDNIGHT DAYDREAMS

MIDNIGHT DAYDREAMS

Poetry of

Heart Tales and

Mindscapes

DOMINIQUE RENDA
BLAKE HORSLEY

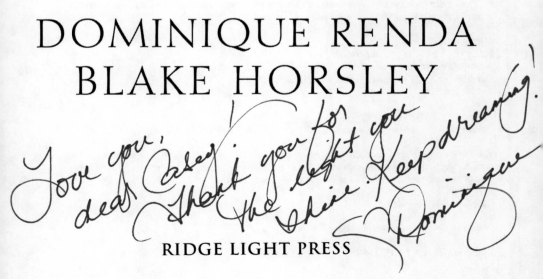

RIDGE LIGHT PRESS

Midnight Daydreams
Poetry of Heart Tales and Mindscapes
All Rights Reserved.
Copyright © 2012 Dominique Renda and Blake Horsley
Ridge Light Press
v3.0

Cover Photo © 2012 Dominique Renda. All rights reserved - used with permission.

ISBN: 978-0-578-10419-5

Library of Congress Control Number: 2012904766

PRINTED IN THE UNITED STATES OF AMERICA

For family and friends,
with love and gratitude.

We are under one sky.

CONTENTS

MIDNIGHT DAYDREAMS

SEATED

Seated in a booth
at our old burger joint,
peanut shells on the floor,
initials carved on the table,
laughter from the crew at the bar,
orders being called from the counter,
late day sunshine pushing in mellow
through weathered shutters and
smoky antique windowpanes,
casting its gold on your soft, silken skin
and prematurely gray-brown hair.

"This is it," you say to me,
and the rustic room falls away,
and the sounds cease to carry,
the patrons change to shadows,
and the light shines on truth,
the aged wood walls listen
while sweet molasses steam pulls back in,
and I am old, old in a moment,
framed in time and stuck to the leather bench
marking the day I sat down to say goodbye to you.

And in quiet mind, I wonder.
How does time trade passion for passage,
and the journey for a mere view?
The heavy doors open,
a couple enters to place their order,
a family exits with a bag of what's left.
"History creates expectation,"
you say to me, your voluntary mother
offering involuntary farewell,
"and expectation makes it so."

Dominique Renda

GOING, GONE

Just like that, overnight,
plus nine days. The berries still
frozen, waiting
to be made into jam, but not today,
not in this house, nor in this town.
She did not want to preserve anything
from summer, or the last three years
before the berries were planted and plucked
in the luxury of time, and a fit of focus.

Just like that, early morning,
minus eight sleepless nights. The dogs loose
in the yard, where else
could they be, when the grand dames strolled by
to investigate the chaos and boxes piled
in the driveway, she expected to answer
questions before they answered their own.

Just like that, one afternoon,
at the end of seven years. She swept up the ashes
from his singed emails to another,
singed emails to a lover,
and brushed them into the soil of the potted gardenia
she would give him. The alluring fragrance of women
bruised with his touch; his alone,
alone with his dogs in the garden.

Just like that, one evening,
the first of all the rest. The car packed, the house clean,
tears shed, few words said, the day now long,
the road longer, she turned the key, glanced out the window,
shifted into first gear and moved on.

Dominique Renda

EVERY AUDREY

Dressed
in casual Hepburn
black, form-fitting
high-neck knit sweater,
loose trousers,
brunette locks in a twist,
silver hoops on her ears,
a delicate watch 'round her wrist.
Breakfast at Tiffany's,
the reservation stands,
but not for this woman,
no ring on her hand.
She likes bright blue ribbons
but boxes repel her,
and suburbs and sneakers,
and men who woo her
because of her beauty
or hand in fine art,
her breeding, the schooling
that set her apart.

One day she crosses the walk
between fantasy and self
and meets the good woman
she'd placed on the shelf
when independence was tearful,
a sadness of its own,
and lonely was too lonely
to be left alone.
Dark days now over,
Audrey in white,
wears linen and sandals,
and dances at night
to the warm island breezes,

the wind at her back,
she moves as she pleases,
unhurried, untracked.

The women, they know her,
and note quite a change,
the ease in her smile,
the gray in her mane.
She laughs with the children,
and brings them supplies,
she speaks with world leaders
and protests their lies.
And when her vast travels
bring her home once again,
she paints a true story
for family and friends.
This is a big life
from both sides now,
and this is a woman
who shares tales of how
to lie down with lions,
and wake up with stars,
and enjoy a fine breakfast,
unreservedly.

Dominique Renda

PENCIL JUICE

Writing at my desk, words flowing fast from
the end of my pencil, spilling over the tablet
into sentences and lines, too many, too fast,
over the sides, over the sides and onto the desk,
onto the desk with lettered-thoughts from
a six-inch wooden spigot, a six-inch wooden
spigot with an open valve lead point,
puddling words, creating a flood, a flood and
a flurry of words in a hurry, rolling down
the side of my desktop. Wiping, writing,
wiping, writing. It's a mess of stories that must
be told, and I can't influence their bold
assertion. Tales poured in words, spilling
stories and slipping subjects, splashing and
puddling onto the floor planks. Thanks but no thanks
for the prolific gift. Too much, too fast, these words,
and what if the spigot is broken. The pencil snaps,
the words slip past the place for writing.
I sponge them up, and mop them up, and start
from the beginning. The end pours first, and works
soaking up the verbiage. The byline claims the name
of the tool whose task is writer.

Dominique Renda

ARTICHOKE

A book with a bad cover
is what I served for supper
but what I ate that night
was not nourishment of the body…
no, not the body but the mind.
That night, as I ate supper,
I explored her many facets.
Just as a book, ever progressing in depth,
I spent dinner trying to peel through
her many protective yet enticing layers.
All in an attempt to reach the heart,
inevitably finding that somewhere
along the way I get hurt.

We come out bleeding,
crying, laughing.
All worthwhile.
I lean back, dumbstruck
by the weight of the
realization:
I have had my lover
for supper.

Blake Horsley

BLENDING INTO BEIGE

"Bifocals," Dr. Wan said to me as she set the frames to rest on the
bridge of my middle-aged nose. "Progressive," Dr. Wan said
as she described the type of lens that would allow this bird her
free range of focus. "What color this time?" asked the sparkling
young assistant wearing hot pink head-to-toe. "May I suggest
beige?"

Beige! Did this visually enthusiastic siren just suggest to me beige?
"Black," I answer, "or red, or green, or silver, or even brown.
Not beige." When did beige become an option, and does one
need an over-fifty prescription for that kind of thing? I leave
the optometrist's office unnoticed by the waiting room of
college students browsing multicolored frames.

Beige! Walking to the train, I notice less space on the sidewalk.
Are my old lean legs taking longer strides, or are young-footed
pedestrians tracking shoes sized like mountains? One
bump-and-shove too many gets a "hey!" from this broad
with corrected vision. "Sorry, didn't see you," brushes my ear
through the thin winter air. I catch the train, unseen by the porter,
and I pay anyway for my seat in the stands.

Beige! I stop at the market; milk and eggs are on my list,
and I add to my basket red apples, bright oranges, and yellow
lemons. I see them clearly through my new bifocals. Though
no one else notices, I am feeling my color.

The walk home from the market is uphill, and my cheeks
are petal-flush. The lantern above my front step glows
golden light, and I slip the key into my cherry red door.

Dominique Renda

UNTITLED 5.

One
Two
Three
Four

One
Two
Three
Four
Reaching out
We fight it

One
Two
Three
Four
Connection
Plop of a drop
Two drops merge into one

One
Two
Three
Four
Rippled surface swelling in all directions
Riding waves of impulse
Across an all-encompassing
Universal water

Waves continue
Unable to slow or stop
Capable only of moving on
Or getting off

Forced to attempt

To derive meaning of
Perplexing images of truth
Racing past in an instant

One
Two
Three
Peering down at the
Mind's mirror
Beneath the surface
Sleeps the reflection
Unconscious true self

Curiosity, wonder
We try to grasp the image
Diluting the liquid truth
Revelation:
Tolerating one's part,
The wave moves on

Four
"Exhale and open your eyes," he says.

Blake Horsley

TALES FROM THE WATCHMAN'S TOWER

It's two in the afternoon before I realize that it has been six
hours since I checked on you, nine blocks cross town, in your
new shiny room, cluttered with new shiny things, including
emails from me. I am keeping an eye on your well-being from
my post in the watchman's tower.

It's earlier than I expected, and you are older than I think. You
laugh like a child, speak as an adult in addled adolescence, leap
onto counters, and swing your arms in expression. The world is
grand, and open, and wide. And I encourage you to engage in it
boldly, and you do. And I see your adventures from
my post in the watchman's tower.

The seasons slip in and slide out, and you cycle the leaf-laden,
well-paved, fast-paced streets of the city we have chosen.
Driving can wait, with its insular power, and tendencies
toward crashing hard. Your own strength takes you to places
best felt from a seat with pedals, smooth wheels, and a flashing
light, which I track through the darkness from
my post in the watchman's tower.

The years are mounting, and the miles expand, and the view
from one corner of land does not provide for the distance
you are ready to go. So I perch tower-top, and ready myself,
ready or not. I want to catch a glimpse of your eyes,
and your spirit and your mood, and have proof
that you are safe, and you are well. I search from
my post in the watchman's tower.

I see less, and close my eyes for quiet prayer. I find you there.
Divine sight, a perfect vision, my vigilant soul can rest
beyond posts in the watchman's tower.

Dominique Renda

SAFE HARBOR

Breathing and sleep
fill the night.
Bass and strings
strum through spring.
Dreaming in Ventana.

Bay window broadly post
foggy sands and bouldered coast.
Morning in Ventana.

Bare feet press hardwood floors.
Arms wrap her waist to touch once more.
Whispers in Ventana.

Crunchy cereal soaked in milk.
Two spoons and kisses soft as silk.
Romance in Ventana.

Wet walks, stretched strides,
silent stories, verbal tides.
Initiation in Ventana.

Poetry, art, and NPR;
creative life near or far.
Home in Ventana.

Dominique Renda

A QUEEN

With her hair slicked back
and all the money in the
world,
with confidence and
joy,
master of her domain,
ruler of her realm.
With her hair slicked back
and all the money in the
world
slept the woman
in her box.

Blake Horsley

SPRING, UNEXPECTEDLY

If it would fall all day, I'd be happy. Light,
damp showers skirting in the petal breeze
of an early morning; leaves caressed
in a mild gust, rustle to a sprinkle.

Spring, unexpectedly!

If it would fall all day, I'd be happy.
Till blossom time – green, vibrant, flourishing –
then leaving me in summer's heat.

Dominique Renda

BOHEMIAN RHAPSODY

It's 2 a.m., always 2,
when I realize sleep
will not come
and I reach for my pen,
this week's smooth favorite,
and a notebook,
this month's hundred pages
of read-between-the-lines, nearly filled,
third week that it is,
and I write rather than smoke and drink,
as he did when it was 2 a.m.,
and I was living between the lines.

A next generation of voices murmur
from the bedroom down a tiny hall,
two husky, playful, tireless teens.
Writing, conferring,
originating their concepts
in lyrics and notes,
rather than poetry and prose,
as their mother does
at 2 a.m.,
creating in the hours
between the lines.

The soft breath of reverie
has rhythm all its own,
drawn in and out
from the youngest child
curled in a cushioned chair
in a room we call ours,
and the place we know peace,
imagination claiming the sense

and experience of merging moments
in a timeless home, at 2 a.m.,
dreaming this reality
between the lines.

Dominique Renda

THE WOMAN WHO LIVED IN TOWN
AND COULD BUY EVERYTHING

The shiny, powder blue Alfa coupe might soon be gone,
but the leather Kate Spade satchel is hers to keep forever.

What of the garden – variegated succulents carefully planted
in imported, glazed ceramic pots, soft pink Amazing Grace
heirloom roses bordering a saltwater spa, and all is surrounded
with freshwater masonry. A painted tile castle made of time
is slipping ground.

Who will rescue her from the hilltop cottage she has yet to acquire,
and what about that trip to the Azores? The paved path pulls away,
the inside track is steep on the curve, and her bare feet are covered
in red dirt. A sober sky hangs blue, a color she calls her own.

Tickling the keys to eastern latches: she has a direction,
if not a home. Imagination designs the footless journey
she travels in moments when the chaos quiets and her
eyes are closed. Jung cycles better answers each time,
and she dreams of doing it right, maybe just once,
maybe always.

Darjeeling or White Tip Earl Grey? She slides back in,
the bouquet of culture and steam return her feet and dreams
to the café on the corner. This is her town. Her eyes are
open, she takes her cup and pays from a limitless Visa.
She is selective; she could buy everything,
though always in a shade of blue.

Dominique Renda

UNDER HOUSE ARREST

Under house arrest.
How does it go?
I sit here at night covered
and coated in white lights
of the Christmas you missed
and I can't go back
to the bedroom at the end
of the hall, where you slept
before your quirky t-shirts
and humor folded
across town through crisscrossed
lines of truth and lies.
A brief hello, a long goodbye.

I wonder still, as night moves
through the frost of holidays lost,
and ordinary days ungathered.
Does time make it better?
Will the house ever warm?
Why must I avoid the back room?

I sleep on a sofa of pillows and
prayers, and ask for forgiveness
for what isn't there. Foggy dawn
greets my melancholy of what
could it be if lines that encircle
brought you to me?

The room's become musty and
the window is cracked. It needs
repairs and new paint for one of
us to come back to life.

Dominique Renda

BOOT BAULKIN'

You sit at the curbside.
You wait at the door.
You stomp your old boots.
You come back for more.

I stand by the window.
I watch through the glass.
I pray for change.
I've learned not to ask.

She has new stories,
and a big-breasted suit.
She wears the pants
to match your old boots.

He whispers softly
and asks me my name.
He doesn't possess me
or point or blame.

These four dance in circles.
They four-square the town.
They welt the floorboards.
They bring the place down.

The spectators clap:
howl, boo, and cheer.
The spectators gawk
and smile in fear.

It could be their turn.
How would they cope?
It might be frightful
to two-step this slope.

Who stops the caller?
Who stops the show?
Who has the courage
to shout what they know?

We don't want the boots.
We can't see through the glass.
We'll pass on the big breasts,
big suit, big ass.

This is a community.
This is a choice.
This is a moment to give
this vote a voice.

We will not sit idly.
We will not watch and hoot.
We will not shake the hand
of the man in killer boots.

Dominique Renda

PINK MOON

Pink moon with yellow glow,
the night is red,
the light is low.
Whispered winds
speak, "Oh, so young."

They kissed first then,
then not 'til noon,
their love too old,
their days too soon.
Four years of courting
to begin.
Time growing long,
time growing thin.

A twilight chance,
the last attempt,
a braided walk
in woven step,
honor held:
a promise kept.
Young romantics turn the cusp
of midnight dreams,
and childlike ways,
and valiant schemes.

The skies loop.
A passage nears:
direction and
commencement clear.

Standing now
in cap and gown,
the sight of two

who turn to catch
a glance, a wink, a handshake,
a breath, a break.

Dominique Renda

UNTITLED 3.

Tales of the other side:
memoir of a cynic.
The world is right,
right enough,
righter than wrong
we see, we react,
and we move on.
One day, one of us,
one of billions, comes to a stop,
to fate, to chance, or to fortune:
unknown, however, never through choice.

Death of optimism:
obligatorily and accidental.
We force, we struggle,
we resist, we attempt to defy.
Fighting: there is no victory or compromise.
We are bent against our will by forces
void of malleability.

This interaction leaves us marked. Tainted,
we emerge.

It started with a girl. It always does.
She used foreign words like:
merr, merp, emoji, and hui,
but then she said goodbye.

And I, I don't know what to do.

Blake Horsley

OUTSIDE THE LINES

The lines are clear:
drafted and drawn
in dismay and discomfort.
The lines fade
with light, and time,
and kindled curiosity.

Too much,
too bright,
no thank you?
Stop? Or

educate, renovate,
dance, climb,
beyond the
borderline.
Discover
intuitive signs

outside the lines.

Dominique Renda

MONDAYS

It happens each Monday morning,
two seasons now, seated in front of the furnace,
seated across from your smile,
a cup of hot water rests
on knees that will not unfold
and stand outside your door.
The black peacoat is stretched on the sofa,
ready, waiting, but not wanting
to leave.

Dominique Renda

HONEY SKIN

Back to the little house this evening.
Cat was out, and I thought: oh no,
another one lost.
Walked through the tiny structure
that was our home
for two days, seven candles,
two and a half meals,
and one shower.
Cups were on the table
next to gifts you gave:
a rock from our walk,
a deck of cards,
and coconut oil
to glaze your honey skin
and berry lips.
Wind whispers through
the scratchy screen door,
blowing open my etched,
autumn heart.

Dominique Renda

WHAT IT LOOKS LIKE

You sit on our common lane, waiting
to ask if I'd like to stroll to the mailbox together.
We do stroll. Halfway down the road you mention
that I am old enough to be a grandmother. It is a stretch,
you say, that I might even be a great-grandmother, if I lived
in another era – say, perhaps The Renaissance, and
another place – say, not Silicon Valley.

We collect our mail. I tuck mine under my arm for the return walk,
and you ask if my back is bothering me, because you think you see
a curvature of my spine which could, one day, without proper
stretching, become a Dowager's Hump like – say, your old
great-aunt Belle, or the woman who sold shoes in the New England
town of your childhood, fifty-four years ago.

You sort your mail while we stand on your front porch discussing
the unseasonably cool weather of these last days of summer. You
remark that women tend to put on a few pounds in cool seasons
and when they age, perhaps as a natural way of insulating through
winter in places such as – say, Siberia, or Nova Scotia, or Vostok
Station, Antarctica. But maybe not in California, you remark,
as I kiss your cheek farewell. And, perhaps it was the bend
of my arm and not a hump, you say, as I say goodbye
and head for my own front door.

And you're not a grandmother yet, you say, as I wave, and wink,
and slip inside the house. And through the open kitchen window
which faces our common ground I hear you ask if I want to get a
bite to eat – say, on the early side? But the Stones are on the stereo,
and it is rather hard to hear you – say, perhaps it is
a senior moment. I know you understand.

Dominique Renda

THE STORY CLOCK

The story clock
ticks off time,
circles hours
no longer mine.
Days once spent
in second hand
now freeze-out
this lived-in man.
I scamper streets
long after dark,
stretching time
to make my mark
on history's record
of what is done
and what is left
for other ones
who run the race
repeatedly
and hold the pace
in spite of me.

Tick-tock,
tick-tock.

The story clock
ticks off time,
circles hours
no longer mine.
Years of tracking
straights and bends,
long hands
fold to make amends
to colleagues,
wives, and old damned dogs

alarmed for me
through the fog of booze
and rants and jobs and raves.
Were they foolish or
were they slaves
to my long stories –
fiction all,
winding tight
this sordid sprawl.

Tick-tock,
tick-tock.

The story clock
ticks off time,
circles hours
no longer mine.
The face is twisted,
the glass is scratched,
the pendulum swings
unattached.
Chimes ring prayer
with grave regrets:
My life's too short.
God, not yet!
Given chance,
and providence,
I will counter
my circumstance.

Tick-tock,
tick-tock.

Breathe.
Breathe.
Welcome faith.
Time stands still.

The clock holds space
for man's free will
to shift direction,
absolve time, and claim
the truth of solid mind.

Tick-tock,
tick-tock.

The story clock
ticks off time,
and minutes, hours
again are mine.
Wonderment and gratitude
move me through the solitude
of sincere lament,
and ripe repent,
and commitment
to do it differently.

Tick-tock,
tick-tock.

The seasons change,
so, too, clocks,
and this man with a reopened heart
meditates and counts my days
by blessing those I scared away.
There is work to do
and I will do it,
paced.

And time will tell.

Dominique Renda

PULLING OUT THE BOTTOM CAN

I said,
"No one ran away today."
Though he did last night.
Down the driveway, never to be seen again,
until four hours later
when he walked back in
because he could, because I was there.
This 17th year, this week, this night,
"Bad?" I asked.
"Yes," he answered,
"but not the bottom of the can."

Dominique Renda

AN ORDINARY MAN

The line at the market is too long
to stand, if standing is an exercise
twenty minutes twice a day;
each day is one more than he'd dreamed of.

The fish dinner prepared fresh
by the woman wearing jeans and an army apron
is fresher than the canned sardines and frozen pizza
dinners he made before she said yes to sometimes;
some time being better than none at all.

The wolf-sleep that comes most nights after
half a bottle of wine, four taped episodes of *Stargate*,
prayers and thanks to whoever brought him out
of the desert and back to the States
is sleep he couldn't reach when peace was beyond
a mined and violent border.

The occasional drivers, paid for their efforts, and a little
extra if they'll hang around and talk for a while,
speak in broken English of a solid America
as home of the free.
Today's freedom cost him a place in the market line,
stability in his home, a solid night's sleep,
and the freedom to walk away from his chair.

Free is what he stands for, and each day is one more day
than he thought he would have when the sand filled his eyes,
and he was airlifted home by another ordinary man.

Dominique Renda

FLOATING ON THE SEA OF MOON

Sea glass and shell trails,
and walking the shore,
a shoe full of sand, a stick in hand,
and six decades of currents
weathered.

Midnight light casts
its white, as ships
slide the seam.
Adventure

and all that we knew
when we said I do
to floating on
the sea of moon.

Dominique Renda

YES, I'LL HAVE SOME SALT WITH THAT

Light and dashing,
he's a shaker:
a bit of bite, and an edge.
He spices it up,
a lot of sparkle and a little pinch,
he captivates my senses.
Rubbed or wrapped:
he preserves the goodness.

A pitcher of water, please.

Dominique Renda

BIRDS OF A FEATHER (LATE SUMMER RANT)

Heavy, rounded, scarlet tomatoes hang
low on twisted and staked, mostly-deep-green vines.
Sun Gold cherry tomatoes garnish three other weighted bushes,
loping on their sides from the multitude of their crop.
Red-veined chard reaches for the late summer sun, nudging
the romaine, green leaf, and arugula lettuces to thrive
in a mere corner of this abundant garden.

Nothing nudges as frequently, and in as many unwanted ways,
as crows. Five slick, black-feathered, pointy-clawed, incessantly
noisy crows, setting up to nest in the large, barely-hanging-on pine
tree shading of an otherwise sunny, summer plot.

Drinkers. I'm convinced these crows are drinkers, marauding
about town long enough to signal to other crows that
the festivities are at my house.

Yackers. They can't seem to agree about anything.
The screeching discussion never ends till nightfall.

Thoughtless. A clean car tagged.

There was a time when the season was new, the tomatoes were
green and the red chard knew its place, the songbirds welcomed
the scene with cheerful greetings; I stretched out in my garden
hammock on a Sunday afternoon, a book in hand and a large
brimmed hat. Peace and pleasure on my own little patch of land.

There was a time, usually 6 a.m., when the nearest neighbor would
brew his pot of hot java, drink two cups, run the local track, and
return in sunrise silence. He brews up targets now: a linear aim
from his upstairs bedroom window to the glossy, black-feathered
screechers perched on a barely-hanging-on pine tree.

There was a time when the tomatoes were juicy, the greens were crisp, and the songbirds chirped from their branch of the barely-hanging-on pine tree, but not now. Not this summertime.

So I guess the party's at my house.

Dominique Renda

GOOSE

Neon beer signs glow warm
red, bright yellow, and Bud blue.
Three flat screens corner the room,
and a fryer press sizzles hot meat
medium rare and ready
for guacamole, bacon, a warm sesame bun,
sweet potato fries, a deviled egg
on the side, and a smile.
"Here you go, Bill, the usual."

A usual beat circles the pool table,
a flap of words and feathers of laughter
circulate between the fans and doors
on Monday night, at the only space,
the home base for a gaggle of men
and women, a flock of kids,
and an endless slog of university students
not far from their nests.

Dominique Renda

WALTZING MATILDA

Wait, wait, I hate to be late
for the gray in my hair
and the key in my skate.
The days move so fast
and the nights move so slow
and I'm asking myself
where did it go.
The years, fifty, and I'm still
twirling thoughts
of what I might do if
I stop laundering socks,
and shuffling through work,
and listening for rain,
and praying for one day
to be just the same as the next
so I will not have to

look up.

Hurry, hurry, I say to myself,
but I'm tired of rushing
to something else
that doesn't come when I want it,
and how would I know; reasons
seem scrambled and hard to
follow through birthdays and tax years
that jump off the books
of weeks and months now recorded,
and spun to their end.
A new calendar opens,
its white pages blinding,
the lines ask for answers,
the answers are crying:

pay attention.

Wandering, circling, I'm looking for me
in a crowd, in a moment,
in my own story
of a woman engaged
in every corner of life:
as a mother, a daughter,
a one-time wife.

And in all this action,
and costs and rewards,
the satisfaction
seems lost to the task
of serving and seeding
and ceasing to pause
for the pleasure of recognizing why
I am here now,
and I am compelled to

breathe.

Breathe. Breathe.
I hold still.
This first time in my life
I surrender,
and ease into
the socks and the rain,
and the taxes the same:
all part of the claim
to days spent as I have chosen.

As I slow the pace,
fifty takes a pause.

Dominique Renda

NINE

It's 9 p.m. and the sun is still
high in the sky
on a hill outside Boise,
over a Walmart parking lot;
farms, fields, and friendly people,
shining 3,000 miles from
the men I dreamed of
twenty years ago on a pineapple island,
in a fair-weathered time,
in a youthful state of a youthful mind.

It's 9 p.m. and the sun is still
high in the sky
on a hill outside Boise.
The horizon is wide and west
and here I put to rest the best
of beginnings, silk and rough waters
between the prairies of what-ifs
and the waves of what-is,
the reasons enough to hold you close,
and let go
of the men I dreamed of
three childhoods ago.

It's 9 p.m. and the sun is still
high in the sky
on a hill outside Boise.
Light-years of bright years and plenty
of grace keep pace with
young men moving in young men time
through seas of changes
and fields of dreams.
This woman beams,

as I stand outside Walmart,
watching passersby,
beneath our shared sky,
and I whisper:
we are together.

Dominique Renda

PHOENIX

The bulb flickers.
The air is still.
The room is silent.
The light dims.
The light dims my eyes, heavy at the rims.
I take a breath, the last.
The room is dark and I am gone.
Body still, the room is filled with chill.
Flick goes the switch and light returns brighter than before.
In pursuit so does my soul rising from the remains:
bright divine glory.
I take a breath, the first.
I am no longer myself, though I remain myself,
risen from the ashes into the glorious new.
The bulb flickers.
The air is still.
The room is silent.
The light dims, and it begins,
begins for all of time.

Blake Horsley

SWEPT

He sits on the bed with tapes telling tales
of witches and dragons, wrapped in a quilt
stitched in stardust, asking me if I had wings
where would I fly, or would a prehensile tail
keep me from falling

in love with his humor and itchy requests
for rest that comes only minutes before
sunrise breaks his fantastical dreams,
decidedly impractical to nonfiction days
and textual tasks piled in calendars

and boxed in thoughts of resigned imagination,
sketched on paper-picked trees, logged below skyline.
He sweeps what remains with a broom
marching out of the closet
while the door swings.

Dominique Renda

WINK AND A NOD

Beautiful. Blink. Grown.
We sit side by side and stretch our long legs
at the same time, in the same way:
ankles crossed, right foot tapping out
that extra energy: our birthright:
happy-tappin'-form.

Beautiful. Blink. Grown.
Shiny dark hair, long and tasseled,
framing angular features and
a beaming white smile.
Slender fingers held gently
in contemplation: strong and soft.

Beautiful. Blink. Grown.
Sparkling almond eyes focused,
shoulders straight, heart astute,
and visible attention is given to
thoughts rolling through.
A clear view of you.

Beautiful. Blink. Grown.

Dominique Renda

SWEET PEA

Dusty days and dry
tree-lined streets unfold
to the laughter and tunes
we whisper and howl
this July evening in a small
college town. The melody and sun
set long after the musician closes
his case of Blue Moon brew
and collected coin. Our dance
has spun twilight, and
at the crosswalk I hear,
"I love you, sweet pea."
It is art, cotton candy
at the carnival, making life
bearable and more: sweet.
A glance, a twirl, the spin.
And why not? We are young
in this light, and we know
we don't need to know.

Dominique Renda

SHADES OF GRAY

Stacks of fashion magazines line the walls.
Pretty heads with cascades of bangs or curls,
but for gray.

Dipped in bowls,
basin-washed,
drained of truth in years now lost,
but for gray.

Tinted and trimmed,
the newly shorn
are dried and styled,
with a youthful air,
but for gray.

Dominique Renda

NEVER TOO LATE TO LEARN

Shallow water.
Toes touching the bottom,
hands gripping the side.

Let go!
Dive into the deep.
Legs and years are long.
The grown-ups are here,
and I am one, swimming in open space.
I can teach you to float, to glide, if you will relax.
But I am in the deep, and your fear of drowning
may hold you
back.

Dominique Renda

MOON ON THE HALF SHELL

The sliver, the edge, the whitest of light,
a crescent, a shadow, a phantom of night.
An onyx sky streaming with purple cast,
a timeless horizon passing fast.

Sprinkled stars in formation,
have stories to share,
a universe listens to
the dog and the bear.

And the old moon sits resting
above and below
the earth and the stars
and mysterious glow

of maroon in the east
stretching up to meet night
and pull back the covers
for morning so bright.

And as it would happen, that slippery old moon
slides off the half shell not an hour too soon.

Dominique Renda

THE SILENT REVOLUTIONARY

One man sitting in a tree,
waiting for the world to change,
contentedly living with his forest elders.
One man with nature, yet part of a greater entity.
One man waving for all his brothers to join him.
We must have infinite faith in each other.
Coming together in the Spartan forest,
becoming more than before.
Rather than love, than money, than fame,
give me truth, demand the woods.
Pure venture into the serenity of thought.
However mean life is, meet it, live it.
Living in the world of peace is one man
sitting in a tree, thinking of a better tomorrow.

Blake Horsley

VERTICAL BLINDS

The sun, it shines just enough, through this mess
of blinds, all at odd angles, vertical, strange, but
they cover, just enough. The light is visible between
slanted strips of protection, distraction, obscurity.
Not really. Inside it is a vertical view out, framing
a horizontal environment. The sun waits, with a
small offering through a sliding, cobwebbed window.

And what of the replacement curtains that were
to be hung before summer? With curtains in place
there would be no peeking. It is a small pleasure
to peek, so the curtains have yet to go up.
It is at night when curtains would be best, preventing
dark views without definition or permission. By day
the sneaky sun shines through slim plastic with
both form and privilege.

And all that may be seen today are shining leaves,
sections of blue sky, and an edge of shingled rooftop.
With just this much information it can be a day
of anything. To see more, would it be less?

Dominique Renda

WHY CLOCKS?

The light casts shadows and the days remain warm,
and I know there is less time forward than back.
Weeks are un-scattered with a million tiny goals, less noisy,
more predictable, and uncertain. Dependable, without
the need to be dependable. Sturdy in a windless sky.

Freshly fallen from a towering lush maple tree,
one variegated green, yellow, and rusty-hued
five-point liquid amber leaf has landed
prematurely, resting on the cobblestone
path, adjacent to a hounding highway where
I walk the old dog.

Messages arrive on a digital screen in a flash
in every moment, in any city, sent from names I'll never place,
and still I look for the white truck and the driver's white
envelopes to be delivered by someone who uses hands
and a map, and arrives at two, once a day, except on Sundays.

No need for my wristwatch, which I used to give up
only on holidays, when time stood still, relaxed
and unaccountable. Now my eyes track forward
what's left behind as minutes shift in data streams.
It would be okay, except I miss the ticking.

Dominique Renda

UPON YES

Love, and colors,
canyon colors –
blues, yellows,
oranges, rusty reds,
sienna, terra-cotta,
river green –
carry me
in rhythm and flow,
weightless in flight,
ascending valleys:
rich, cool, fresh
beginnings.
Smooth rock,
palm to stone, toes to ledge –
knowing, centered,
beauty rising
and eagles soar.
Single tree
on crescent peak –
a nest, bright bounty, blue,
breathing,
I am here:
One
with sky and light
and birds in flight
and love has brought me
to Yes.

Dominique Renda

COFFIN

Here I am, here I lie
in this coma of life,
slowly I sink in the despair of the couch
while a paradigm of darkness reigns.

Ceiling in my eye
while nothing surrounds me.
Desperately I try to escape
the life I find myself chained to.
I have become the wrath of my existence,
searching for the door, a door.

Soon time runs out on my wrist:
looming future and eternal despair.

The sanctuary of the night nears its end.
Shackled in the body and tortured in the mind
I retreat in desperate longing.

A hollow corpse in the darkness.

Stumbling the way to my closet
I abandon sanity and religious ration.
Stripping myself bare, slowly
I edge to my coffin: Eden's salvation,
confined in constriction,
with nose to knee,
for unspoken hours.

But I am safe,
except for the inquisition of my mind.

Blake Horsley

AND SO

And so,
here I am again, at Waddell State Beach,
spring waves crashing and churned,
a horizon wide and vague as imagination.
People scattered on the sand and shore
like odd-chipped sea rocks exposed to wind,
cold, and dogged flies.

Watching with curious eyes.
It makes me shiver; it makes me hot.
It makes me weary till I rest.
I cannot breathe, but then I do.
Salty air fills my chest.
A child toe-tips in the surf,
feeling warm, feeling safe,
standing in organic grace.

I watch and question this weathered place.
Year after year the tide rolls in,
boards, sails, and playful travelers
out for fun. Relaxed, undone.
I wonder what brings us back
to rocks, water, and blown-out days,
mist, sun, perpetual haze.
Is it the broad-beach, or the closeness
of elements under toe and overhead?

These impressions move past stories read.
It makes me think, it makes me dream.
It touches my skin and blows in my ears.
And so I walk the glistening shore,

and understand my wish for more,
and I and others return each spring
to Waddell State Beach,
unquestioning.

Dominique Renda

DO YOU CRY?

When the timing isn't right, but he is
the one you would want to know better,
better than he was when he slid
down the highway, tripped on your doorstep
and couldn't get up, like he had been – up,
before you knew him, before work ceased and illness
named what would be the end, ending faith
that was his salvation. When redemption was more
than prayer plucked on a six-string guitar, or
more than a story of when. When he asked you
to remind him how to dance and how to play,
but you weren't there when, and you never knew
how, and the best you can do now is hang up
old photos and write a new song while the clock ticks
backward, and louder, and wrong. You ask
if he can make that damn clock stand still.
He says that he will in a few days, a week or two,
maybe in a few months. The calendar moves
while you stand in one place, and the stillness is
you staring down fate. The man is the bundle
you wished to arrive with a package of life,
a lifetime to build it, and redemption
in his fingertips. Now his fingers strum your arm
as you hold his cheek in your hand. This
is your time. Is this redemption? Do you cry?

Dominique Renda

EASY

The half-moon gently suspends midnight,
pinning a dark-draped backdrop behind a speckled stage,
diamond dazzlers, and powder white wisps of cumulus cotton.
Drifters and diehards, the night knows them well.

Quiet is broken; a chirp of perched mockingbirds
hail sneaky morning to slide under the moonlit sky.
Dawn defers, raising her silky slip of pink and peachy edges
atop a ridged and silhouetted horizon.

Pastel light peeks and presses across the landscape,
and a blinding burst of yearning yellow melts
into cornsilk blue, with a promise:

More.

Dominique Renda

IF WISHES WERE HORSES

The sound of running water
through the pipes, over
the driveway, into the creek.
You, seated at your desk,
then working in the garage,
crafting shelves, making spaces.
I watch the faces of the children,
our friends, your smile. I wait
a while before doing the dishes
and restacking books, folding laundry
and paying bills. Time stands still.
A radio plays the old tunes,
Mama's voice tells a tale
of beggars and horses
and natural forces
befallen to wishers
and dreamers' high rides
left to dandelions and stars,
now not as far
as the man in Levi's
and the woman with a pen.
There is no end.
Home is created,
the water runs through,
beggars ride bareback
and dreams do come true.

Dominique Renda

DOG DAYS

Even now, even here, even forty years later,
there is a calm to things: the '70s summer feeling.
Free-and-easy, summer hits its stride:
tall plastic glasses
of cold old-fashioned drinks,
watermelon women wearing skimpy clothing,
marshmallow men in generous smiles.
"Honey, how 'bout a stroll tonight?"

A simple pace past stretched
berry-brown arms and lanky legs
hanging over deck chairs, fence tops, porch steps;
giggles in gardens and parked cars,
among crickets and night birds,
and welcome breezes;
box fans and ice buckets on counters,
and books strewn over cool corners;
bodies swaying and snoozing, slung
in crescent canvas hammocks.

Sirius sky, bright-eyed, sparkling tail,
through forty rollovers of
blazing days and panting nights.
Lists of odds-and-ends never end
and in the end, all is equal.
A lovely, mellow, quirky state
of something cool and groovy,
and even now, even here,
the dog days track us home.

Dominique Renda

VENUS WISHES

And on this night I send you light
and hope the world spins left to right
for all the women who dance 'til dawn
and all the men who smile upon
the brave idea that God above
may shine on them as female love
and if they do, and if they might,
make a wish on Venus bright,
in western sky, held mid-height,
for all to see and dream their best
for happiness and all the rest
then let 'em dance and let 'em smile
and God will be there all the while.

Dominique Renda

THERE'S A WORD FOR IT

Waking up in circles of hot, warm, and cold,
I am aware of the time, and confused about the place.
I know it is Monday, and I am eight or fifty. It's all the same
on the inside, at sunrise, when I am still half asleep.
In the night I hand in a poem to my second-grade teacher,
and today it will be submitted to the magazine
before noon, as promised to a friend who writes opera
and transplants azaleas in her Darwinian garden. It's now
or never she says, before the gorilla chases her back
into the kitchen. Words are the difference because they remain
ours in the garden, or in the kitchen, in the classroom
and on the page. At any age, language makes us human,
and speaking keeps us sane; the schoolgirl and the poet
use words to explain their perspective on the heat,
and big monkeys in the yard, and the questions
of writing something that takes us further.

Dominique Renda

EVENTUALLY A SHOWER, BUT FIRST THIS

Balmy, summer nights dreaming
the hours rather than sleep,
until another day just like this one.

California mountaintop,
soaked Sierras whisper and cry
through rocky ridges and
boundless meadows. Tioga Pass
weaves a stony passage.

Broad-day breezes brush my arms.
Orchards and dairy farms,
sandy deserts, small towns,
long empty roads, highways and trails,
and turnoffs for stretching, eating apples,
and making love.

The view from a big sky:
golden blends with a blue
and generous horizon.
This supple land holds its people while
daylight-dreamers touch the earth.

Reading roadmaps
of refuge in the rain,
bikers and store owners have it all:
bugs and beans and gourmet chocolate.
Living heaven in high water,
stormy winds, peaceful seas, dusty paths,
and a rolling ride home.

Dominique Renda

About the Authors

As poet, author, and fine art photographer, Dominique Renda's distinctive written and visual images capture the purity and presence of the human condition. A graduate of the University of California, Los Angeles, and CTI international Leadership Program, Dominique has written creatively and professionally for more than two decades. As a photographer, Dominique has been a featured artist exhibited in San Francisco, Silicon Valley and Los Angeles. Midnight Daydreams is her third published book of poetry.

A young poet and filmmaker, this collection represents Blake Horsley's first published poetry. A lifelong collector of stories in all genres, Blake explores the intersection of truth in art. As a student, an observer, and raconteur, Blake creates narratives to provoke consideration and promote understanding.

Also by Dominique Renda

*String of Lights – Poetry and Photographic Art
of the Human Landscape*

*Dominique Renda and Brooks Anderson
Mirror Publishing*

*Swimming in Open Water – Poems and Photographic Art
of Fluid Transition*

*Dominique Renda and Brooks Anderson
Between Waters Publishing*

CPSIA information can be obtained at www.ICGtesting.com
Printed in the USA
LVOW090732180812

294741LV00002B/13/P